DATE DUE

Dr. Anthony Kooiker.

University of Edinburgh

The Russell Collection
and other Early Keyboard Instruments
in Saint Cecilia's Hall
Edinburgh

Edinburgh University Press

©   Department of Early Keyboard Instruments 1968
Faculty of Music
University of Edinburgh
Edinburgh University Press 1968
22 George Square
Edinburgh 8
85224 047 3

Library of Congress
Catalog Card Number 68 – 8905

Printed at The Curwen Press

Contents

Virginal. S. Keene 1668, no. 8

Foreword

The late Raymond Russell F S A, F T C L, was a man of many
interests, an expert collector of early medical books, an
antiquarian occupied in his last years with researches concerning
Malta, and throughout his life a devotee of the harpsichord. His
collection of keyboard instruments was assembled up to about
1958, at various times including instruments which, after careful
study, he subsequently sold. He gradually brought his collection
to a high degree of selectivity, his two dozen instruments
covering two and a quarter centuries and five countries.

By 1958 when engaged on his book *The Harpsichord and Clavichord*
(Faber & Faber, 1959), he conceived the ideal of his collection
becoming a permanent 'live' museum in association with the
Faculty of Music of a British University. Negotiations with
Edinburgh University in 1959 remained only tentative until an
adequate building was found. Late in 1959 there came the
opportunity for the University to acquire the St Cecilia's Hall
buildings. These comprised (i) the Hall designed by Robert
Mylne for the Musical Society of Edinburgh, built in 1762 and
used by that Society until the end of the century–a first-floor
hall, originally oval, with a 'Laigh Room' below; (ii) the
Freemasons' Room adjoining the Hall on the first floor, built by
them in 1812 during their ownership (1809–44) when they
converted the hall into a rectangle; (iii) adjoining small premises
to the north thrown in during the nineteenth century; and (iv)
the premises (originally shops) beneath the 1812 room. The
University commissioned Mr Ian Lindsay to restore the Hall
and to adapt and extend these buildings to provide a Department of Early Keyboard Instruments. On Mr Lindsay's
death in 1966, Mr John Reid of Ian Lindsay and Partners
assumed the responsibility for completing these plans.

On the early death of Mr Raymond Russell in 1964, his mother
Mrs Gilbert Russell presented the greater part of his collection

Harpsichord. S. Bolcioni 1627, no. 4
See also half-title for detail of bentside

to the University of Edinburgh 'in memory of her son and to fulfil a wish long entertained by him', as is recorded on plaques in the two galleries. The gift also included Raymond Russell's note-books and his complete collection of photographic negatives and prints covering both his own and other collections.

It had originally been intended that Mr Russell would prepare two catalogues – a brochure for the use of visitors to the collection, and a large-scale definitive catalogue fully illustrated and documented. The present booklet is the brochure, a full catalogue being envisaged for future publication.

In compiling the brochure we have drawn upon Mr Russell's archives mentioned above, and have received assistance and information from Mr W. R. Thomas, Mr J. J. K. Rhodes, Mr John Barnes and Mr Christopher Shaddock; also from Mr Robert Goble and Mr Trevor Beckerleg, the restorers of certain instruments. The 'Notes on the Makers' (pp. 65–9) are based partly upon the data published by Mr Donald Boalch in 1956, but incorporating adjustments. Finally, we must thank Mr Tom Scott for the skill and artistry which he has so successfully applied to the difficult task of photographing this collection.

In accordance with present-day practice, all measurements are given in centimetres.

Sidney Newman
Peter Williams

Painting on wing lid of Ruckers Harpsichord 1608, no. 3

Notes

The *Russell Collection* of nineteen instruments comprises nos. 1–15, 18–19, 21, 22. The complete collection is not arranged chronologically in the two galleries; with some exceptions, the first gallery (Freemasons' Room) is devoted to English instruments with mahogany cases. Visitors desiring to follow a fairly chronological sequence starting with the early instruments are advised to begin at the far end of the New Gallery.

References in the text are to the following books:

BOALCH: *Makers of the Harpsichord and Clavichord, 1440–1840* Donald H. Boalch (London 1956)

GROVE: *Grove's Dictionary of Music and Musicians*, 5th edn. (London 1954). Numbers refer to the catalogue entries given there under the makers' names

HIPKINS: *History of the Pianoforte* A. J. Hipkins (London 1896)

HUBBARD: *Three Centuries of Harpsichord Making* Frank Hubbard (Cambridge, Mass. 1965)

RUSSELL: *The Harpsichord and Clavichord–an Introductory Study* Raymond Russell (London 1959)

Index to Countries

The Catalogue

The rose from the Orlandus spinet 1710, no. 11

Pentagonal Spinet or Virginal

1   *A. Bertoloti 1585*

A very fine Italian *spinetta* of a type now called *virginal*,
because both nut and bridge are fixed to the soundboard.
Nameboard inscribed

ALEXANDER BERTOLOTI. F. M.D.LXXX.V.

Instrument and soundboard of cypress in a separate outer case.
Wrestplank not original. Natural keys of boxwood with arcaded
fronts; accidentals, of American black walnut, not original.
Rose (9·3 cm) of Gothic tracery.

Dimensions
instrument 160·0 (greatest) × 38·1 (greatest) × 17·1
outer case 166·4 × 52·7 × 19·7
key lengths 10·8 *c.* 6·8
keyboard width: total 70·8, c–b² 50·2

Specification. C/E–f³, 50 notes, with provision for extra string
playable by key C/E and tuned to suit musical requirements.
One set of strings, 8′.

Decoration. The jack rail and mouldings are studded with ivory,
as are now the fronts of the natural keys. The outer or carrying
case, a typical Italian device, was originally painted black. Later,
a hood was cut, with music painted inside; the hood was
abolished and the music fitted as a flap but upside down. The
inside of the lid was painted with a hunting scene to which was
added the central group of figures, the outside case lacquered
bright blue and later overpainted green, at which point the
pair of stools was provided.

History. Bought by Hugh Gough in 1951, restored by him
and sold to R. Russell. Restored by W. R. Thomas and
J. J. K. Rhodes in 1968.

References. Boalch, no. 2; Russell, p. 36 and plates 9 and 10.

Harpsichord

2 Italian c. 1600

A good example of an Italian 'continuo harpsichord'.
Instrument of cypress in a separate outer case resting on two
pedestals of convential thick-strap design. The music desk is
modern. Rose (12 cm overall) with open centre. Natural keys of
ivory with shallow arcaded fronts, accidentals of dark wood
inlaid with three stripes, light wood between ivory.

Dimensions
instrument 188·6 × 78·4 × 20·0
outer case 195·6 × 87·0 × 23·5
key lengths 9·3 5·7
keyboard width: total 69·9, c–b² 48·9

Specification. C–d³, 51 notes. The top five accidentals are built up
of originally split keys, as also the key-plates of C♯ and f♯; this
probably indicates an original keyboard with split D♯/E♭ and
G♯/A♭ in middle and lower part of the compass with perhaps a
broken octave bass. Two sets of 8¹ strings, originally (?) with
metal knobs to the slides protruding in the short side of both
instrument and outer case. Stop levers not original. The lowest
five strings are carried on their own bridge-section. The hitch-
pins of the lowest 19 strings are fixed into the outside of the
instrument case, the strings passing through holes in the side
of the case and round another set of pins before passing to the
bridge pins. The nut is fixed to a small second soundboard set
over the wrestplank.

Decoration. The outer case is painted with a large scrolled-leaf
design, gold on green background. The inside of the lid has a
painting of a glade with Apollo and the Nine Muses.

History. Restored by Leslie Ward in 1948.

Reference. Hubbard, p. 24, footnote.

Two-manual Harpsichord

3   Andreas Ruckers the Elder 1608

An instrument showing changes to which many harpsichords have been subjected. Name batten (not original) inscribed
ANDREAS RUCKERS ME FECIT ANTVERPIAE 1608
Date on soundboard, 1608. Rose (6·5 cm), harp-playing angel between initials 'A. R.'. The seventeenth-century framed stand with six square tapered legs is probably Flemish, perhaps original. Modern keys with naturals of ebony, accidentals topped with ivory.

Dimensions. Instrument 223·5 × 80·0 × 26·7
key lengths: upper manual 10·1 5·6   lower manual 10·5 5·8
keyboard width: total 72·0, c–b² 48·9

Specification. GG/BB–d³, 51 notes, no c♯³. Three sets of strings, 8¹ 8¹ 4¹ (originally 8¹ 4¹). The restored jack slides protrude through the short side in the following order from back to front:
    lower manual 8¹ (buff plectra)→
             8¹→
             4¹←
    upper manual 8¹←   The upper keyboard slides for coupling.

Decoration. The outside is painted green with gold scrolled-leaf borders. The oil painting on the wing lid, an amorous scene, is signed 'P.C. IV' on the upper edge of the closed book depicted, perhaps PIETER CODDE (1619–66). The painting on the flap lid is a classical scene of amours. The characteristic Ruckers *tempera* flower painting on the soundboard is all but obliterated. The lining papers to the keyboard surround are modern.

History. Originally a 'transposing harpsichord' like the Jan Ruckers of 1638 (see no. 6), it was later rebuilt with two manuals of the same pitch. In the eighteenth century it was converted into a pianoforte and the upper keyboard removed. About 1928 Alec Hodsdon restored it as a harpsichord with a new upper keyboard. Bought by R. Russell in 1952. Restored in 1953 by Andrew Douglas with new keyboards and jacks, the original lower keyboard being preserved (see exhibit 3 A).

References. Boalch, no. 72; Grove, no. 1.

3 A   Original lower keys and keyboard frame of exhibit 3. The original compass of C/E–f³ has been altered to C–d³ chromatic.

Three-manual Harpsichord

4   S. Bolcioni 1627

A much-altered instrument of deceptive appearance. Back of nameboard (from another instrument?) inscribed STEFANUS. BOLCIONIUS. PRATENSIS. F. A.D. M.D.C.XXVII.F. Instrument of cypress; rose (11·7 cm overall) of wood and parchment. Natural keys of walnut plated with ivory, accidentals of stained wood inlaid with ivory slip.

Dimensions
instrument 200·7 × 78·7 × 22·4
outer case 215·9 × 87·0 × 25·0
key lengths: top and middle manual *c*. 8·4 *c*. 4·7
                 bottom manual *c*. 8·8 *c*. 5·2
keyboard width: total 69·6, c–b² 47·0

Specification. C/E–g³, 52 notes. Three manuals, probably French, from a genuine three-manual harpsichord. At present unstrung, but the three manuals are meant to play one set each, 8¹ 8¹ 4¹ from bottom to top, the two upper manuals united by a sliding coupler. The present instrument is composed of harpsichord parts from several countries and periods, the 'original' instrument probably containing one manual and two sets of strings, 8¹ 8¹. Formerly, a short octave of pedal pulldowns was fitted (holes drilled through case) and the original instrument probably had a compass of 53 notes. The keyframe is modern as is the coupling device. Wrestplank and bridges were inexpertly made for conversion to a three-manual instrument.

Decoration. The instrument rests in an Italian outer case with rich French decoration on gold ground, the lid interior with figures in a lake-side scene. The elaborately carved frame stand (nineteenth century?) with eight legs and understretcher is closely similar to that depicted in Georg Kinsky *History of Music in Pictures* (1930) p. 125, no. 1.

History. Restorers include A. N. Masson (1915) and M. Asseman, whose signatures appear on the instrument. In 1930 owned by M. and A. Salomon (Paris).

References. Boalch, no. 1; Philip James *Early Keyboard Instruments* (London 1930) p. 125 and plate XLV; Russell, pp. 29, 30, 36, 144.

Harpsichord

Jan Ruckers 1637

A good example of a single-manual Ruckers, one of the most
important types of harpsichord. Name batten inscribed
JOANNES RUCKERS ME FECIT ANTVERPIAE 1637
Date, 1637, painted on the soundboard. Rose (7·2 cm) 'I.R.'
('2nd type'). The ivory natural keys and ebony accidentals are
English eighteenth-century work, as are about half the jacks.

Dimensions
instrument 184·8 × 84·4 × 24·2
key lengths 12·7 8·3
keyboard width: total 78·6, c–b² 48·8

Specification. A A–f³, 57 notes, the original compass being at
least 48 notes, probably from C. During the eighteenth century,
the instrument was subjected to 'ravalement', that is, the
widening of the whole instrument – case, soundboard, etc. – in
order to extend the treble compass. Three sets of strings, 8' 8' 4'.
Stop knobs are:

    left 4' (back register)→   *inner right* 8' (front register)→
                                       outer right 8' (middle register)←

Before the 1952 restoration a pedal worked the 4' by means of a
pulley (still present). The inside right lever and knob are
eighteenth century.

Decoration. In the eighteenth century, the case was lacquered red
with gold leaf-patterned bordering. The lid flap has an oil
painting of a woman (St Cecilia?) at the organ. The soundboard
is decorated in *tempera*; the decorated wrestplank is modern. A
portion of the dowelled extension to the original wrestplank is
preserved separately as exhibit 5 A.

History. Formerly owned by J.C.Horsley RA. Restored by
Hugh Gough in 1952. Bought by R.Russell in 1953. Restored
by John Barnes in 1968.

References. Boalch, no. 59 and plate VII; Grove, no. 17. The
instrument was depicted in an oil painting by W.P.Frith RA
(1819–1909) which was sold at Sotheby's in June 1946.

Two-manual transposing Harpsichord

6 Jan Ruckers 1638

A unique surviving example of an unaltered transposing double harpsichord. Very many, though not all, double-manual harpsichords built before 1640 were of this type, although subsequent alterations have generally disguised this fact (cf. no. 3 above). Transposing harpsichords enabled players to accompany in two of the several pitches in use at the time.
Name batten inscribed

JOANNES RUCKERS FECIT ANTVERPIAE

Date, 1637, painted on the soundboard. The note names written by the maker on the wrestplank are a rare feature. Rose (9·5 cm), not original, probably Italian. Natural keys of bone, accidentals of black wood.

Dimensions
instrument 223·5 × 78·7 × 26·3
key lengths: upper manual *c.* 9·7 *c.* 6·2
                 lower manual *c.* 10·2 *c.* 6·5
keyboard width: total upper manual 64·5, c–b² (both) 50·0
                     total lower manual 71·6

Specification. Upper manual: C/E–c³, 45 notes ('standard' Ruckers pitch). Lower manual: C/E–f³, 50 notes, aligned so that keys F–f³ play the same strings as the upper manual keys C–c³, five extra sets of strings being provided for the additional lower manual keys. Key C on the lower manual therefore plays a string tuned a 4th below key C on the upper manual (GG). Two sets of strings, 8' 4', now missing, played from both manuals. The slides protrude through the right short side in the following order from back to front

     lower manual 4' ←
                8' →
     upper manual 4' ←
                8' →

Buff batten (harp stop) for the 8' (divided at c♯¹/d¹).
Two features complicate the transposing arrangement:
mean-tone tuning made it necessary to have two strings for

d♯/e♭ and two strings for g♯/a♭ (since mean-toned e♭ on the upper manual would be too sharp to serve for the g♯ key on the lower); and short-octave compass meant that the bottom F♯ and G♯ keys on the upper manual would be in the wrong order for playing the D and E strings on the lower manual unless constructed to pass over F and G.

Decoration. Inner surfaces are lined with original Ruckers' papers. The flowers and fruits, etc., painted on the soundboard, are characteristic. The lid interior has a fine oil painting of a landscape with figures.

History. Previous owners were: E. Spence (Florence), before 1896; Sir Bernhard Samuelson (England), sold 1915; Mrs Lotta van Buren Bizallion who loaned it to Yale University. Bought by R. Russell before 1956.

References. Boalch, no. 61; Grove, no. 19; Hipkins, pp. 87–8; Hubbard, pp. 63–71; Sibyl Marcuse 'Transposing Keyboards on Extant Flemish Harpsichords' *Musical Quarterly* XXXVIII (1952) 414–25 (2 plates); Russell, pp. 44–5 and plates 33–5.

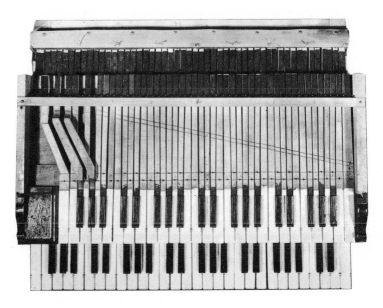

Harpsichord

7 J. Couchet 1645

The oldest surviving instrument by a maker commonly accredited with important developments to the Flemish harpsichord. Name batten and jack rail both inscribed
JOANNES COUCHET FECIT ANTVERPIAE
Soundboard and jack rail dated 1645. Rose (7·6 cm), 'I.C.' The eighteenth-century keys have naturals of ebony with moulded boxwood fronts and accidentals topped with ivory.

Dimensions
instrument 181·6 × 70·5 × 24·2   key lengths 11·5 7·3
keyboard width: total 67·0, c–b² 47·9

Specification. Four octaves, C–c³, 49 notes, original compass uncertain. 'Ravalement' was carried out in the eighteenth century (see no. 5) but the instrument was subsequently restored to its original size. Three sets of strings, 8¹ 8¹ 4¹ (at present it is unstrung), stop knobs placed above the keyboard. The second 8¹ was added probably when the compass was enlarged.

Decoration. The soundboard and wrestplank are painted in *tempera* with flowers, etc.; the inside of the case and the keyboard-surround are lined with paper of scrolled design and medallions. The case is painted green with gold moulding at the lid edge. The inside of the wing lid has the initials 'R.L.' above a trophy.

History. Bought by R. Russell from E.C. Legg and Son.

Virginal

8   *S. Keene 1668*

A fine example of the late English rectangular virginal, with the standard rich decor of the period. Jack rail inscribed
STEPHANUS KEENE LONDINI FECIT 1668
The oak coffer case has a convex lid with steel strap hinges; the oak stand is modern. Four roses, three in main soundboard (5·1 cm, 7·6 cm, 6·4 cm) and one behind wrestpins (7·6 cm). Natural keys of dark stained wood with gilt embossed fronts, accidentals of ivory.

Dimensions
instrument $182·2 \times 55·2 \times 25·4$
key lengths *c.* 9·0 *c.* 5·5
keyboard width: total 71·1, c–b² 48·6

Specification. FF–d³, 57 notes, no FF♯. One set of strings, 8¹.

Decoration. Inside the lid, a park or lake-side scene, painted in *tempera*, with figures in the foreground; inside drop-board a similar scene, partly obliterated. Embossed gilt paper (or leather) on front panels and lining the inside; studding of ivory or bone.

History. Formerly at Goodrich Court, Ross-on-Wye. Bought by R. Russell in 1949. Repaired by Leslie Ward in 1950.

References. Boalch, no. 1 and plates XXIII–XXV; Russell, plates 57 and 58.

Bentside Spinet

9 *English, late seventeenth century*

A spinet of unusual hexagonal shape, halfway between the pentagonal and bentside spinet. In England, the wing-shaped spinet began to supplant the rectangular virginal from about 1670, until in the eighteenth century it became the standard English domestic instrument.

The case is of walnut. Natural keys of black wood, accidentals of ivory. Signature on bottom and (original) top keys, 'T.A.'. The nameboard has an early example of marquetry; the stand with turned legs is original.

Dimensions
instrument: spine 149·9, depth 16·5
key lengths 8·8 5·7
keyboard width: total 70·7, c–b² 47·9

Specification. GG/BB–d³, 54 notes. Keys C♯ and D♯ are split to provide two notes each (AA, C♯ and BB/D♯). Compass originally extended only to c³. One set of strings, 8¹.

History. Formerly owned by the artist T.B. Hardy. Bought by R. Russell in 1952. Restored by Robert Goble and Son in 1967.

Reference. Russell, plates 59 and 60.

Bentside Spinet

10 T. Hitchcock c. 1705

An English spinet of uncommon double-bentside shape.
Nameboard inscribed

THOMAS HITCHCOCK LONDINI FECIT NI241

On back of nameboard is scratched '1241T(7)'. On lowest key
'Will Hilliar Haris No 7'. On top key '7 Hilliar'. On bottom
jack is stamped 'H7', which also appears on front of wrestplank.
'54' is scratched on header. Lowest key bears pencil inscription
'HW 88'. The case is solid walnut, the keyboard surround, jack
rail and lining veneered in figured walnut with herringbone
banding. Natural keys of ivory with arcaded fronts, accidentals
of ivory between ebony sides ('skunk-tail' design).

Dimensions
instrument: spine 177·8, depth 17·0
key lengths 10·7 6·5
keyboard width: total 83·2, c–b² 48·3

Specification. Five octaves, GG–g³, 61 notes. One set of
strings, 8¹.

History. Formerly at Goodrich Court, Ross-on-Wye. Bought by
R. Russell in 1955. Restored by Robert Goble and Son in 1967.

References. Boalch, no. 8a; Russell, plate 65.

Ottavino or Octave Spinet

11 *P. M. Orlandus 1710*

A very small triangular spinet of a type popular throughout the
period, pitched to sound an octave higher.
Nameboard inscribed
DV̄ VIXI TACVI MORTVA DVLCE CANO
  [Whilst living I was silent. Now dead I sweetly sing]
Inscription on back of nameboard probably copied by
Mabel (?) Dolmetsch, possibly from original jack rail
PETRUS MICHAEL ORLANDUS ANNO 1710
Case, painted dark green, lined with cypress, the soundboard of
pine; the stand is modern. The rose (9·8 cm) of parchment is
exceptionally intricate. Natural keys of boxwood, the name-
letters written on the keys in ink; accidentals of stained wood.
Wire loops are fitted to the case, presumably for a carrying strap.
At the top right of the nameboard is lightly scratched, in an
Italian hand, lettering which appears to read 'Genoal conto'.

Dimensions
instrument 83·2 × 79·7 × 14·0, depth 14·0
key lengths 7·5 4·3
keyboard width: total 62·1, c–b² 48·3

Specification. Four octaves, C/E–c³, 45 notes. One set of
strings, 4ˡ.

History. Restored by Dolmetsch. Bought by R. Russell in 1956.
Restored by John Barnes in 1967.

Harpsichord

12　T. Hancock 1720

A very rare example of an early eighteenth-century English harpsichord, showing certain Italian characteristics – scaling, diagonal jack slides, double unison strings. Nameboard inscribed

THOMAS HANCOCK LONDINI FECIT 1720

The case has veneered walnut sides and a solid walnut lid, the interior banded with a double line in black. Mahogany front board and jack rail not original. The stand, with five square tapered legs, is from a later date. Natural keys of ebony stripes between ivory sides.

Dimensions
instrument $210 \cdot 8 \times 90 \cdot 8 \times 20 \cdot 3$
key lengths $11 \cdot 3$ $7 \cdot 0$
keyboard width: total $79 \cdot 7$, c–b^2 $49 \cdot 3$

Specification. $GG–e^3$, 58 notes. Two sets of strings, 8^1 8^1 (now mostly missing). The stop levers are of steel, protruding through the nameboard.

History. Formerly at Cobham Park, Kent (The Earl of Derby). Bought by R. Russell in 1957.

References. Boalch; Russell, p. 74.

Bentside Spinet

13 J. Harrison 1757

Nameboard inscribed
JOANNES HARRISON LONDINI FECIT 1757
Bottom and top jacks stamped 'A.P.'; on bottom key in ink
'Arch. Pringle 1757'; also on top key without date. Mahogany
cross-banded case; lid with modern walnut veneer strengthening
inside. Original stand with turned legs. Natural keys of ivory
with moulded ebony fronts, accidentals of ebony (?).

Dimensions
instrument: spine 177·8, depth 20·0
key lengths 12·2 7·8
keyboard width: total 83·8, c–b² 48·9

Specification. Five octaves, G G–g³, 61 notes. One set of
strings, 8¹.

History. Repaired by E. C. Legg and Son in 1954. Bought by
R. Russell in 1955. Restored by Trevor Beckerleg in 1966.

References. Boalch, no. 2; Russell, plates 69 and 70.

Harpsichord

14 J. A. Hass 1764

A unique and very important German instrument.
Soundboard inscribed

J. A. HASS HAMBG ANNO 1764

The case of mahogany veneer set in herringbone pattern was restored in 1935 when probably the six fluted legs were fitted. The soundboard, with floral decoration, has no rose. Natural keys of ivory, accidentals of black wood (both replated *c*. 1840?).

Dimensions
instrument 231·1 × 97·8 × 24·2
key lengths 13·7 9·1
keyboard width: total 84·4, c–b² 49·3

Specification. Five octaves, FF–f³, 61 notes. Three sets of strings 8¹ 8¹ 4¹. The stop levers on the wrestplank (not protruding through the nameboard) are
   outer left 8¹ (front register) →
   inner left 8¹ harp (back register) ←
   inner right 8¹ (back register) ←
   outer right 4¹ (middle register) →

History. From a letter of C. J. Reinhold (Amsterdam 1867), whose grandfather had owned it, the instrument appears to have belonged to Mozart and to have been carefully restored about 1840. From 1867 to 1937 it was owned by members of the Six family of Amsterdam. After extensive renovation by Erard in 1935, it was bought in 1937 by Miss Mary Dunne of California who loaned it to various museums, and was purchased from her by Raymond Russell in 1955.

Reference. Boalch, no. 18, plates XVII and XVIII.

Two-manual Harpsichord

15 P. Taskin 1769

An exceptionally fine and important instrument of the
fully-developed French type. Inscription painted round the rose
PASCAL TASKIN ELEVE DE BLANCHET
Date, 1769, painted on the soundboard. Rose (8·2 cm),
harp-playing angel between initials 'P.T.'. Natural keys of ebony
with pale wood arcaded fronts, accidentals ivory topped.

Dimensions
instrument 231·7 × 93·1 × 27·9
key lengths: upper manual 10·7 6·7
               lower manual 11·3 7·4
keyboard width: total 81·9, c–b² 46·7

Specification. Five octaves, FF–f³, 61 notes. Three sets of strings,
8' 8' 4' with buff batten (harp stop) for both 8' choirs. The upper
keys slide in for coupling. The 4' jacks lie between the two 8'.
The four stop levers, placed above the keyboard, are
    left lower 8' ←   *centre* upper 8' (harp) →   *right* lower 4' →
                     lower 8' (harp) ←

Decoration. The outside of the case is pale green lacquer with
gold-band panelling; the inner surfaces are pale chocolate lacquer
with gold bands. The original framed stand has six cabriole legs,
painted as the outside of the case. The soundboard and
wrestplank are painted in *tempera* with flower sprays.

History. Russell bought the harpsichord in Paris in 1952, at
which time Mme Arlette Taskin, a descendant of the Blanchet
and Taskin family, recounted that it had been her father's
property and that it had been restored in 1882 by Louis
Tomasini, whose inscription may be seen stamped on the
wrestplank. On the death of M. Taskin, it was bought by the
pianist Louis Dièmer (1843–1919) who had frequently borrowed
it for concerts in Paris. During the German occupation of the
Second World War it was temporarily moved to Vienna. Russell

has noted that after the 1882 restoration 'it was lent to Erards who wished to copy it for commercial production, and with this modern harpsichord-making began'.

References. Boalch no. 1 and plate XI; Hubbard, pp. 118–22, 130, and plate XII; Russell, pp. 59, 60, and plates 47, 48; Russell 'The harpsichord since 1800' *Proceedings of the Royal Musical Association* (1955–6) p. 64.

Two-manual Harpsichord

16   J. Kirkman 1773

A typical example of a fully-developed English harpsichord.
Nameboard inscribed

JACOBUS KIRKMAN LONDINI FECIT

Case of mahogany banded with light wood; original stand with
four turned legs. Rose (8·3 cm), Orpheus between initials 'I.K.'
Back of nameboard signed in pencil 'XVIII Jacobus Kirkman'.
Underside of soundboard (before being glued down) signed in
pencil 'Robert Falkener London Fecit 1773 September'.
Natural keys of ivory with arcaded fronts, accidentals of ebony.

Dimensions
instrument 241·3 × 99·1 × 29·2
key lengths: upper manual 11·6 7·2
                    lower manual 12·8 8·2
keyboard width: total 83·2, c–b² 48·8

Specification. Five octaves, FF–f³, 60 notes, no FF♯. Three sets of
strings, 8' 8' 4', with lute (upper 8'), harp (lower 8') and
machine stop. The hand stops were originally

> *outer left* lute 8' →   *centre* harp 8' ←   *outer right* lower 8' ←
> *inner left* 4' →   *inner right* upper 8' →

The two left-hand stops are now dummies. The machine stop,
added at an early date, has a unique system of two pedals

a.   both pedals in raised position
> *lower manual* 8'+4'+upper 8'
> *upper manual* 8'

b.   left pedal depressed
> *lower manual* 8' only
> *upper manual* takes off 8', brings on lute

c.   right pedal depressed followed by left pedal
> *lower manual* leaves on 4' but takes off both 8'
> *upper manual* takes off 8', brings on lute

Further changes of tone are made possible by removing the iron
taper plugs connecting lever with register.

History. Probably owned originally by General John Reid
(1721–1807) who bequeathed his instruments to Edinburgh
University with effect from 1839. Restored by W. R. Thomas and
J. J. K. Rhodes in 1953.

Bentside Spinet

17 *Baker Harris 1776*

An English spinet of unusually rich tone. Nameboard inscribed
BAKER HARRIS LONDINI FECIT 1776
Case of mahogany banded in fine lines of light wood. Natural
keys of ivory with moulded fronts, accidentals of ebony.

Dimensions
instrument: spine 185·4, depth 20·5
key lengths 12·7 8·5
keyboard width: total 82·9, c–b² 48·3

Specification. Five octaves, FF–f³, 60 notes, no FF♯. One set of
strings, 8¹.

History. Probably owned by General John Reid (see no. 16).
Restored by W. R. Thomas and J. J. K. Rhodes in 1952.

Reference. Boalch, no. 13.

Bentside Spinet

18   N. Stewart 1784

Nameboard inscribed
NEIL STEWART EDINBURGH FECIT
Date, 1784, is stamped on bottom key. Bottom key and bottom
jack stamped '3', which is also written on various parts of the
interior. Back of nameboard signed in ink 'AR for NS 21',
interpreted to be 'Andrew Rochead for Neil Stewart'. (For
Rochead see no. 25). Case of highly-figured mahogany panels
with cross-banding, the lid in plain mahogany. Natural keys
of ivory with moulded fronts, accidentals of ebony.

Dimensions
instrument: spine 188·0, depth 21·0
key lengths 12·1 7·7
keyboard width: total 82·9, c–b² 48·6

Specification. Five octaves, FF–f³, 61 notes. One set of strings, 8¹.

History. Formerly at Goodrich Court, Ross-on-Wye. Bought by
R. Russell in 1955. Restored by Trevor Beckerleg in 1967,
including new nut and jack rail.

Reference. Boalch, no. 2.

Harpsichord with swell

19 J. Broadwood 1793

Nameboard inscribed
JOHANNES BROADWOOD HARPSICHORD 1793 NO 1155
GREAT PULTENEY ST. GOLDEN SQUARE
This is the last recorded number and date of a Broadwood
harpsichord and the only instrument inscribed by Broadwood
alone. Case of mahogany, panels lined with boxwood binding
and surround cross-banded in mahogany. Music desk not by
Broadwood. Natural keys of ivory with moulded boxwood
fronts, accidentals of ebony.

Dimensions
instrument 231·1 × 94·0 × 29·8
key lengths 12·5 7·7
keyboard width: total 83·5, c–b² 48·9

Specification. Five octaves, FF–f³, 61 notes. Three sets of
strings, 8' 8' 4', with lute, harp, machine stop, and Venetian
swell shutters. The stop knobs above the keyboard are
> *outer left* lute→   *inner right* 8' (quill plectra)→
> *middle left* 4'→   *outer right* 8' (leather plectra)←
> *inner left* harp (8')←

The machine is activated by a brass stop to the left of the
keyboard
> *left pedal* reduces from full to leather 8', or to lute, or to both
> depending on which registers have been set.
> *right pedal* operates Venetian shutter swell.

History. Formerly at Blüthner's Perivale workshops. Bought
from Dolmetsch by R. Russell in 1955.

References. Boalch, under 'Shudi' no. 1155; Russell, pp. 81,
88, 94.

Two=manual Harpsichord

20   R. *Goble and Son 1967*

Robert Goble's 'Concert harpsichord' with five-octave compass, four sets of strings (16¹ 8¹ 8¹ 4¹, lute, two harp battens, coupler), half- and full-notch foot-levers, plastic jacks and leather plectra. Case of figured walnut. Bought by the University in 1967.

Dimensions
instrument 243 × 99·1 × 28·5
key lengths: upper manual 11·2 6·7
             lower manual 12·8 7·8
keyboard width: total 83·5, c–b² 48·8

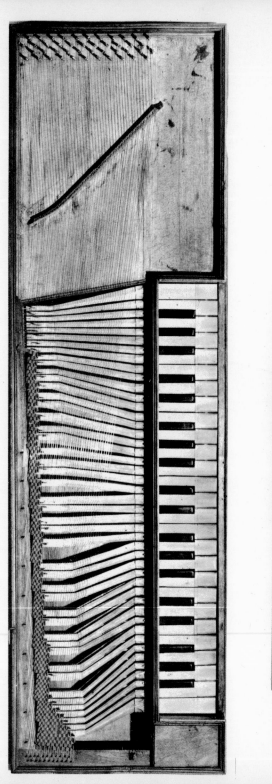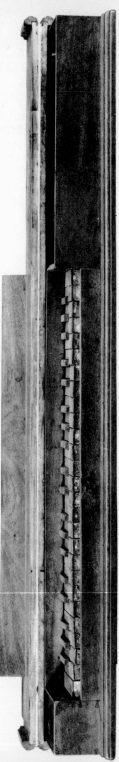

Fretted Clavichord

21 German (?) c. 1700

A small, undecorated clavichord of an inexpensive, portable type. Instrument of walnut and soundboard of spruce, the lid, of pine, fitted with a parchment hinge. The stand is modern. Natural keys of yellow-toned wood with embossed leather fronts, accidentals of white wood plated with black varnish.

Dimensions
instrument 106·7 × 31·1 × 8·9
key lengths 8·3 5·0
keyboard width: total 62·0, c–b² 48·3

Specification. Four octaves C/E–c³, 45 notes. The twenty-two pairs of strings are played by the following notes
C, D, E, F, G, A, B♭–B♮, c–c♯, d, e♭–e♮, f–f♯, g–g♯, a–b♮, c¹–c♯¹, d¹–e♮¹, f¹–g¹, g♯¹–b♭¹, b♮¹–c♯², d²–e♮², f²–g², g♯²–b♭², b♮²–c³.

History. Bought by R. Russell about 1958. Restored by John Barnes in 1967.

Unfretted Clavichord

22 J. A. Hass 1763

A large and unusually important German clavichord.
Soundboard inscribed

J. A. HASS HAMBG ANNO 1763

Natural keys of tortoise-shell with arcaded ivory fronts,
accidentals of ebony plated with mother-of-pearl. The stand,
with cabriole legs, is modern.

Dimensions
instrument 173·3 × 53·3 × 17·4
key lengths 12·9 8·4
keyboard width: total 84·4, c–b² 49·3

Specification. Five octaves, FF–f³, 61 notes. Double strung
throughout (8' 8') with a third set of strings (4') FF–B.

Decoration. The decoration is unusually sumptuous, the exterior
lacquered in red, black and gold, with *chinoiserie*, the interior with
olive-wood veneer, mother-of-pearl, and *tempera* designs
(soundboard), while inside the lid is an oil painting of a river
scene.

History. Formerly owned by Lord Dartmouth, and Captain Lane,
Wanstead. Bought by R. Russell in 1956.

References. Boalch, no. 15; Russell, pp. 100, 103, and plates
93, 94.

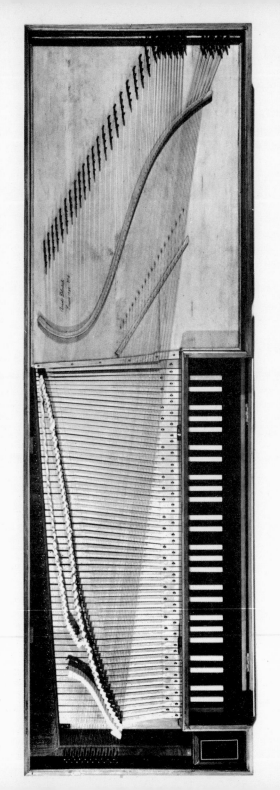

Unfretted Clavichord

23 A. Dolmetsch 1896

An early modern clavichord, probably modelled on an instrument made by C. G. Hoffmann in 1784 which Dolmetsch then owned. Nameboard inscribed

ARNOLD DOLMETSCH LONDON FECIT M.DCCC.XC.VII NO 6

Case of Oregon pine with elaborate brass hinges; soundboard of spruce signed 'Arnold Dolmetsch London 1896 No 6'. Natural keys of ebony, accidentals of boxwood.

Dimensions
instrument $172 \cdot 7 \times 53 \cdot 3 \times 16 \cdot 5$
key lengths $13 \cdot 0$ $8 \cdot 7$
keyboard width: total $84 \cdot 2$, $c-b^2$ $49 \cdot 3$

Specification. Five octaves, $FF-f^3$, 61 notes. Double strung throughout (8^1 8^1) with a third set of strings (4^1) $FF-c$.

History. Owned by the University since about 1900.

Grand Pianoforte

24 A. Backers 1772

An important early grand piano. Nameboard inscribed.
AMERICUS BACKERS NO 21 LONDINI FECIT 1772
Case of mahogany, banded in boxwood and rosewood, the
wrestplank veneered in sycamore; the stand, with four legs and
understretcher, is original. Rose (7·0 cm), entwined 'A.B.' in
scroll pattern. Natural keys of ivory with moulded wood
fronts, accidentals of ebony.

Dimensions
instrument 224·8 × 92·7 × 27·9
key lengths 12·3 7·9
keyboard width: total 83·2, c–b² 48·8

Specification. Five octaves, FF–f³, 60 notes, no FF♯. Double-
strung throughout. Three hooped metal plates arch from
wrestplank to front of soundboard (a structural reinforcement);
above them is a 'damper rail'. The hammers, all of the same
size, have rolled leather heads, thicker for the bass register. The
dampers (to d³ only) are stiff wires carrying cloth rings. Two
pedals operate through the shafts of the two front stand-legs:
the left pedal moves the keyboard to the right for *una corda*, the
right raises the dampers. The action is very similar to
'Broadwood's Grand Action'.

History. On continuing loan to the University by His Grace
the Duke of Wellington.

Square Pianoforte

25 A. Rochead c. 1805

Nameboard inscribed
ANDREW ROCHEID AND SON
   Greenside Place, Leith Walk, Edinburgh
Case of mahogany edged with satinwood, the keyboard surround
with satinwood and fretwork panels. The framed stand has four
tapered legs. Natural keys of ivory with moulded boxwood
fronts, accidentals of ebony. Number on board at bass end
'368'. Signature on key rail at bass end 'M 2 b d NP'.

Dimensions
instrument $162 \cdot 6 \times 59 \cdot 0 \times 24 \cdot 2$
key lengths $12 \cdot 3 \quad 7 \cdot 8$
keyboard width: total $93 \cdot 3$, $c-b^2$ $49 \cdot 3$

Specification. $FF-c^4$, 68 notes. Double-strung throughout, the
lowest seven double strings overspun. The hammers, hinged
with leather, have oval heads. The dampers, released by the
pedal, operate from below the strings. The action is
'Broadwood's Single Action'.

History. Owned by the late A. Harry Hodge (Edinburgh) and
presented to the University by Mr James Hodge in 1963.

Cabinet upright Pianoforte

26   *J. Broadwood 1834*

Nameboard inscribed
JOHN BROADWOOD AND SONS / Makers to His Majesty and
the Princesses / Great Pulteney Street, Golden Square / LONDON
Number inscribed on wrestplank 'c 1668' (the date 1834 was
verified by the firm before its archives were destroyed by fire).
Case of rosewood inlaid with brass; spiral pillared legs below
keyboard. Natural keys of ivory, accidentals of ebony.

Dimensions
instrument $179 \cdot 1 \times 114 \cdot 3 \times 58 \cdot 4$
key lengths $13 \cdot 3 \quad 8 \cdot 8$
keyboard width: total $100 \cdot 5$, $c-b^2$ $49 \cdot 0$

Specification. Six octaves, $CC-c^4$, 73 notes. Double strung
throughout. Two pedals operate the dampers (right) and
felt strip (left).

History. Formerly owned by the Danish concert pianist August
Hyllested (d. 1946). Presented to the University by Professor
Sidney Newman in 1968.

Chamber Organ

27 English, late 17th century (?)

A small chamber organ with wooden pipes characteristic of English work at the time of Bernard ('Father') Smith. Natural keys of ebony, accidentals topped with ivory. The keyboard resembles those made by Snetzler and was probably added in the eighteenth century.

Dimensions
instrument 199·4 × 99·7 × 54·6
key lengths 11·8 7·4
keyboard width: total 69·6, c–b² 49·3

Specification. C–d³, 51 notes, C♯ key plays AA. Three and a half ranks of pipes: stopped 8¹, open 4¹, open 2¹, open 4¹ (from c♯¹). The second 4¹ rank was added in 1965: its metal pipes are held in a previously empty rack. Pipes c²–d³ of the 2¹ rank were remade in metal in 1965. The six iron stop levers are

left Fifteenth→	*right* Octave (new 4¹)←
Principal Bass→	Principal Treble←
Diapason Bass→	Diapason Treble→

The ranks halve at c¹/c♯¹. Electric bellows-blower since 1965; original iron bellows-pedal (still operative) on the front lower case. At one time the organ may have had a composition pedal.

Decoration. Case now painted in light greys. The paintings of King David and St Cecilia on the inside of the doors are probably nineteenth-century classical pastiche.

History. Built for a small church in Gloucestershire (Cherington (?) near Avening) possibly by 'Father Smith' (according to nineteenth-century tradition). It suffered dismantling and severe damage until it was eventually rebuilt by J.W.Walker for the Reverend A.H.Frost. In 1882, it passed to the uncle of Mr T.W.Hirst of Fairlie House, Ayrshire, by whom it was presented to the University in 1952. It was restored by Noel Mander in 1965.

Chamber Organ

28 J. Snetzler (?) c. 1750

A large chamber organ of unusually fine tone characteristic of certain English builders, with a mahogany case resembling the work of Johan Snetzler. Natural keys of ivory, accidentals of ebony.

Dimensions
instrument 312·4 (including pediment) × 144·8 × 68·6
key lengths 12·1 7·3
keyboard width: total 79·5, c–b² 48·8

Specification. GG/BB–e³, 54 notes, with E♭ but no BB. Four and a half ranks of pipes, stopped 8' 4' 2⅔' 2', open 8' (from c¹)
    left Twelfth   *right* Fifteenth
       Stop Diapason   Principal
       Open Diapason
Electric blower, 1967; original back bellows preserved as reservoir. Composition pedal to the sliders, which, while depressed, takes off all ranks but the Stopped Diapason 8'.

Decoration. Classical broken pediment above the case; panels with dummy gilded metal pipes and scrolled floral designs.

History. Built for the Earl of Normanton, at Ditchley, near Woodstock, Oxfordshire. Bought and restored by Noel Mander in 1967. Bought for the St Cecilia Hall by the University with the aid of a Government grant.

Note on the Early Organs in St Cecilia's Hall

Source: the *Sederunt Books* of Edinburgh Musical Society, preserved in Edinburgh Public Library, vol 11 p. 164 (January 1766) and pp. 167, 173, 175, vol. 111 pp. 176–7 and the entries for 6 April 1768, 22 December 1768, 12 March 1773 and 24 June 1776.

From 1764, probably until the new organ was ready in 1775, the Society used an organ brought from Craigforth, near Stirling, the home of John Callander (1710–89), musical antiquarian and member – perhaps founder-member – of the Scottish Society of Antiquaries. The *Sederunt Book* entry for 19 June 1764 contains in the accounts for the year 1763–4 the charges for packing, carriage and 'setting up of the organ', the last by a Mr Johnston for £5 10s. This sum suggests a small chamber organ, though one large enough to be dismantled when moved. On the analogy of similar musical societies in England, it can be supposed that the Edinburgh Society needed an organ both for *continuo* or accompanimental purposes and for solos in such works as the organ concertos popular from the 1740s onwards. Only Edinburgh residents who had travelled south would have associated the organ with church or church services.

After much correspondence on the society's part, and great delay on Snetzler's, a new organ was built and set up in 1775 by Snetzler, in an alcove at the performers' end of the Hall. Its stop-list probably followed closely that suggested by the publisher-contractor Robert Bremner in 1773

Compass, $GG–e^3$ (57 notes?)
Open Diapason	8^1
Stopped Diapason	8^1
Dulciana	8^1
Principal	4^1
Flute	4^1
Fifteenth	2^1

Sesquialtera (bass Mixture)
Cornet (treble Mixture)
The whole contained in a Swell box worked by a pedal-lever.

In 1765–6 the suggested scheme had included a reference to the

◄ The chamber organ (no. 28) shown in the Saint Cecilia's Concert Hall

Swell mechanism: '. . . a pedall to play Forte and Piano and to
Swell the whole organ.' This device may have been an early
Venetian Swell (see instrument no. 23) or perhaps more likely
some sort of 'sash-window', consisting of a box whose front
panel could be raised by pulley. At this point, there was also
keen interest shown in a stop called – with some degree of
self-deception – *Violoncello*. This was probably not a reed stop,
as it would have been in a Venetian organ of the time, but a rank
of narrow-scaled cylindrical metal pipes, called *Salizional* in
central Europe and *Dulciana* in those organs Snetzler had once
known in Austria.

In about 1800, the 1775 Snetzler organ was 'transferred to the
Assembly Rooms, George Street . . . and was finally taken down
to be employed, as far as might be, in other instruments seven
or eight years ago' (Sir J. G. Dalzell *Musical Memoirs of
Scotland* 1849, p. 132).

24 *Americus Backers*, a Dutch *émigré* working in London, was one of the most important builders experimenting in pianoforte actions. James Broadwood writing in 1812, attributed the invention of the grand pianoforte as he knew it to 'Americus Baccers' in 1772, the date of the instrument exhibited here. Backers's mechanism is called the 'English grand-pianoforte action'.

1 *Alexander Bertoloti*, a Venetian builder of whom little is known. The 1585 virginal has his name spelt thus, while a harpsichord of 1586 in the Brussels Conservatoire has *Bortolotti*: probably an altered inscription.

4 *Stefano Bolcioni*, of Prato near Florence, is recorded as living in Florence in 1634, while a reference to *Stefano Folcione* in Prato in 1641 probably relates also to him. One other harpsichord ascribed to him is dated 1631 and is preserved at Rhode Island School of Design.

19 *John Broadwood*, 1732–1812, born at Cockburnspath,
26 Berwickshire, moved to London as a joiner in his twenties, and from 1761 worked for *Burkat Shudi* (see *Jacob Kirkman* below). From 1770, their harpsichords bore the double signature of Shudi and Broadwood, although after 1773 the Shudi concerned was *Burkat Shudi II* (son of Broadwood's master). In 1795 the firm became John Broadwood and Son, later Sons. The last recorded harpsichord of the firm was no. 1155, made in 1793 and signed by Broadwood alone. From 1773 Broadwood had also been building square pianos, and from 1781 grand pianos.

7 *Jan Couchet*, d. 1655, was the nephew of *Jan Ruckers* (Hans the Younger) with whom he worked for sixteen years. A master of great repute, he continued the traditions of the Antwerp builders, developing various aspects of harpsichord construction; but to accredit him with the invention of the second, non-transposing manual is misleading. His three sons all became members of the instrument makers' Guild of St Luke.

23 *Arnold Dolmetsch*, 1858–1940, born at Le Mans, descended from a long line of professional musicians. After studying in Brussels, where he met Dièmer (see no. 15) and London, where he made his first clavichord in 1894 and harpsichord in 1895, he worked in Boston, USA, for the firm of Chickering 1905–9, and in Paris for Gaveau 1911–14. In 1914 he resettled in England at Haslemere, establishing workshops from which have stemmed several English makers, including *Robert Goble* (no. 20).

16 *Robert Falkener, Falkner* or *Ffalknor* was a London harpsichord-maker resident in 'Salisbury Court, Fleet Street' according to the *London Universal Directory* of 1763. A few other references in this period relate to this obscure builder, including an action against him taken by *Jacob Kirkman* in 1771.

12 *Thomas Hancock*, spinet- and harpsichord-maker in London. His only known surviving instrument is this very interesting harpsichord of 1720, similar in some respects to the two-manual instrument by *Thomas Hitchcock* in the Victoria and Albert Museum.

17 *Baker Harris*, fl. 1740–80, instrument-maker in London, produced spinets, harpsichords, organs and pianofortes (the last from at least 1772). Some fifteen spinets and one harpsichord are known to survive, dating from 1740 to 1777.

13 *John Harrison*, harpsichord- and spinet-maker in London. The six recorded spinets date from 1749 to 1781. *Archibald Pringle*, a workman whose signature is found on the spinet of 1757, was building in his own right by 1765.

14
22 *Johann Adolph Hass*, fl. 1740, died before 1790, was a member of a well-known family of instrument-makers in eighteenth-century Hamburg. Four of the harpsichords by J. A. Hass's father, *Hieronymus Albrecht Hass*, have survived–three of them with original 16^1 stops, two with original 2^1 stops and one with three manuals; of J. A. Hass, the only survivor is this single-manual harpsichord. Eighteen clavichords of the Hass family still exist; they are usually, as here, decorated most sumptuously.

10 *Thomas Hitchcock* was the name of two, possibly three builders, working in London during the end of the seventeenth century and the beginning of the next. The second or third builder of this name was apprenticed to Benjamin Slade in 1700, the family probably numbering its instruments continuously: no. 1425 is dated 1733 and the numbers continue until at least no. 1547. No. 2012 was made by a John Hitchcock (d. 1774). Some twenty harpsichords by '*Thomas Hitchcock*' survive. Workmen's signatures include 'James' and 'William Hilliar' (the latter in no. 1425).

16 *Jacob Kirkman* or *Kirckman*, 1710–92, was born *Jakob Kirchmann* at Bischweiler near Strasbourg. In about 1730 he came to England and worked for *Hermann Tabel*, marrying his widow in 1738. Tabel was a Flemish *émigré*, having learnt the art from the later Antwerp builders and evidently passing on their traditions to both Kirkman and *Burkat Shudi* (founder of the house of Broadwood). By 1772 Kirkman had taken into partnership his nephew Abraham Kirkman, 1737–94, whose son Joseph joined the firm in 1789 and carried it on from 1794. Of the large number of harpsichords which the Kirkmans built, at least 105 are known to survive, rather more than half of which have two manuals.

8 *Stephen Keene*, *c.* 1640–1719 or later, was apprenticed to Gabriel Townsend in London; in 1662 he became a freeman of the Joiners' Company and in 1704 Master. Of the nineteen known instruments by him, seventeen are wing-shaped spinets while only two are virginals (1668, 1675). The extant rectangular virginals of English make all cover the period 1641 to 1679; none are older, although two of the nineteen are undated.

11 *Petrus Michael Orlandus* has left no evidence of his work except this *ottavino* of 1710, the inscription presumably copied by a member of the Dolmetsch firm from an original signature.

18
25   *Andrew Rochead* was a 'musical instrument maker, back of weigh house', i.e. Castlehill, Edinburgh, according to the Edinburgh Post Office Directory of 1793/4. In the following years' lists, the name changes from the original form 'Rouchead', to 'Rochead' and 'Rocheid'; the 1814/15 Directory adds 'maker to his Royal Highness the Prince Regent'. A later firm, P. C. Roughead, can be traced from 1842 to 1905.

3
5   *Ruckers* or *Ruckaerts* is the most famous name in harpsichord-making; a family of masters working in Antwerp
6   from 1573 (or earlier) for about a century. The best-known members were *Hans the Elder* (*c.* 1550–*c.* 1625), his sons *Hans the Younger* (1578–1643) usually known as *Jan*, and *Andreas the Elder* (1579–1651 or later), the latter's son *Andreas the Younger* (1607–67 or later), and *Christophel* whose dates and relationship are uncertain. There are about 140 instruments claiming to come from their workshops: 4 *ottavini*, 41 virginals, 6 double virginals, 25 single-manual harpsichords, 53 double-manual harpsichords and 3 harpsichords with *ottavini* built into the right-hand long side. Many of their much-prized harpsichords underwent almost total rebuilding in the eighteenth century, often at the hands of the finest Parisian masters such as *Blanchet* and *Taskin*.

27   *Bernard Smith*, usually known as 'Father Smith', may have been an English builder who learnt his art in Friesland, rather than a Dutch or German-born builder, as was formerly thought. The many chamber and church organs he built before his death in 1708 were famous for their well-voiced, sweet brilliance of tone.

28   *Johan Snetzler*, 1710–85, was a German Swiss *émigré* who brought to England in the early 1740s certain characteristics of South German and Austrian organ-building. The clear, robust tone of the organ in the present St Cecilia's Hall is less typical of his instruments than the list of stops contracted for in the original organ of 1773–5 (see p. 63).

18 *Neil Stewart* was music-publisher and dealer in Edinburgh, first recorded in 1759 and from 1787 called Neil Stewart & Co. Evidently *Andrew Rochead* did work for him, as did *James Logan* in 1774 (one recorded spinet). Several London publishers at this period also put their nameboards on instruments made for them by other (sub-contracted?) builders.

15 *Pascal-Joseph Taskin,* 1723–93, was born at Theux near Liège, Belgium. He moved to Paris as a young man and worked under *François-Etienne Blanchet* (d. 1761) and his son *François-Etienne the Younger* (1730–66). When the latter died in 1766, Taskin married his widow and succeeded to the business. Taskin's nephew, also named Pascal-Joseph, married his uncle's step-daughter and from them the Taskin family descended. Although Taskin was the most famous French maker of the later eighteenth century, only five instruments built by him are still known. Much of his fine work went into the rebuilding of early Flemish harpsichords. Six such rebuilt instruments of Taskin were amongst the sixty-two confiscated from the Parisian nobility during the French Revolution, deposited in the Paris Conservatoire (founded 1795) and chopped up for firewood in 1816.

		FF	GG	AA	C
1	Virginal by Bertoloti, 1585 C/E–f³, one 8ˡ				128·8
					24·2
2	Anonymous harpsichord, *c.* 1600 C–d³, longer 8ˡ				153·0
					14·3
3	Harpsichord by Ruckers, 1608 GG/BB–d³, longer 8ˡ, 4ˡ				
	longer 8ˡ		166·4		164·2
			13·7		13·3
	4ˡ		94·6		92·0
			6·4		6·4
4	Harpsichord by Bolcioni, 1627 Present approximate scale of one 8ˡ row				141·6
5	Harpsichord by Ruckers, 1637 AA–f³, longer 8ˡ, 4ˡ				
	longer 8ˡ			142·5	136·7
				15·2	15·0
	4ˡ			79·2	74·2
				12·0	11·3
6	Harpsichord by Ruckers, 1638 Transposing manual, C/E–f³, upper manual, C/E–c³. The lower manual plucking points are 2·5 cm (8ˡ) and 3·5 cm (4ˡ) longer		lower manual C (GG)		
	8ˡ		169·5		167·0
			17·4		14·0
	4ˡ		95·9		93·3
			8·9		5·4

	c¹	c²	c³	d³	e³	f³	g³
09·0	62·8	33·0	16·2			13·0	
27·9	15·5	8·6	7·9			8·4	
01·0	51·8	26·5	13·0	11·3			
12·7	11·5	9·0	6·7	6·2			
23·8	71·1	35·6	16·8	15·8			
9·5	7·3	5·1	3·8	3·5			
61·6	33·0	16·5	7·6	7·6			
4·8	3·8	3·3	2·9	2·8			
		36·2					13·3
00·9	64·0	34·5	17·8			12·5	
13·0	11·8	8·2	6·0			4·8	
53·6	33·3	17·0	9·9			6·2	
10·4	8·9	6·9	5·3			4·5	
19·7	70·5	35·6	17·4				
11·5	8·9	7·0	5·3				
52·3	34·6	17·4	8·2				
5·1	4·1	3·5	2·8				

		FF	GG	AA	C

7 Harpsichord by Couchet, 1645
C–c³, longer 8¹, 4¹

	FF	GG	AA	C
longer 8¹				141·0
4¹				76·2

8 Virginal by Keene, 1668
FF, GG–d³, one 8¹

	FF	GG	AA	C
	162·6			135·9
	15·2			11·8

9 Anonymous spinet, late 17th century
GG/BB–d³, one 8¹

	FF	GG	AA	C
		130·8		127·6
		11·2		10·2

10 Spinet by Hitchcock, c. 1705
GG–g³, one 8¹

	FF	GG	AA	C
		151·2		143·5
		17·8		20·6

11 Ottavino by Orlandus, 1710
C/E–c³, 4¹

	FF	GG	AA	C
				74·3
				5·4

12 Harpsichord by Hancock, 1720
GG–e³, longer 8¹

	FF	GG	AA	C
		163·2		152·1
		17·4		16·6

13 Spinet by Harrison, 1757
GG–g³, one 8¹

	FF	GG	AA	C
		148·6		134·6
		15·6		16·2

14 Harpsichord by Hass, 1764
FF–f³, longer 8¹, 4¹

	FF	GG	AA	C
longer 8¹	181·9			169·8
	16·8			15·2
4¹	121·3			100·2
	10·5			9·5

15 Harpsichord by Taskin, 1769
FF–f³, longer 8¹, 4¹

	FF	GG	AA	C
longer 8¹	176·3			162·6
	16·2			14·3
4¹	108·0			89·9
	8·9			8·6

c	c^1	c^2	c^3	d^3	e^3	f^3	g^3
111·1	69·6	34·9	17·8				
54·6	31·1	18·8	7·9				
91·4	55·9	31·1	17·8	15·5			
10·8	7·0	5·7	5·4	5·1			
90·8	48·9	25·7	12·1	10·2			
8·9	7·0	6·1	4·4	4·4			
103·2	52·1	27·6	13·7				9·5
17·1	13·7	10·2	6·4				5·1
57·2	33·6	16·8	7·6				
5·1	4·4	4·1	3·1				
91·7	49·6	24·8	12·4		9·8		
14·0	11·5	8·4	5·7		5·1		
95·3	53·3	26·0	12·7				8·2
17·1	14·9	9·8	5·1				3·8
118·4	69·4	36·9	18·3			14·0	
12·7	10·2	7·6	5·4			4·1	
65·4	34·6	17·1	8·9			6·7	
7·9	6·4	4·7	3·1			2·5	
114·3	67·9	34·0	17·8			14·9	
11·8	9·2	7·0	5·1			4·4	
61·0	33·6	15·2	8·2			7·0	
7·3	5·1	3·9	3·3			3·1	

		FF	GG	AA	C
16	Harpsichord by Kirkman, 1773 FF, GG–f³, longer 8¹, 4¹				
	longer 8¹	182·9			168·6
		18·8			17·1
	4¹	107·3			91·4
		11·8			9·8
	plucking point of lute	7·6			6·7
17	Spinet by Baker Harris, 1776 FF, GG–f³, one 8¹				
		153·7			143·3
		17·1			19·6
18	Spinet by Stewart, 1784 FF–f³, one 8¹				
		156·5			144·4
		16·2			18·0
19	Harpsichord by Broadwood, 1793 FF–f³, longer 8¹, 4¹				
	longer 8¹	184·2			167·0
		20·6			18·8
	4¹	102·2			86·4
		11·8			10·8
	plucking point of lute	11·2			9·8
20	Harpsichord by Goble, 1967 FF–f³, 16¹, longer 8¹, 4¹				
	16¹	183·5			175·0
		23·6			22·7
	longer 8¹	178·2			170·5
		12·7			12·0
	4¹	124·5			116·0
		7·3			6·9

c	c¹	c²	c³	d³	e³	f³	g³
118·7	66·0	34·9	18·1			14·3	
13·7	10·5	8·6	7·0			6·4	
60·3	32·1	15·3	7·6			6·5	
7·6	5·7	4·7	3·5			5·1	
4·4	2·8	1·7	1·6			1·4	
93·5	52·7	26·4	12·5			9·5	
19·3	17·6	12·7	6·5			4·4	
100·4	51·8	25·0	13·0			10·7	
17·5	15·0	11·2	6·0			4·7	
120·0	69·9	34·9	17·8			13·3	
15·2	12·4	9·5	6·7			7·0	
59·7	34·0	16·8	8·2			6·7	
8·6	8·2	7·0	5·4			5·1	
7·6	6·1	4·1	2·5			1·6	
135·5	89·0	45·5	26·4			22·4	
21·1	19·6	18·2	16·7			16·0	
133·5	87·2	43·1	22·3			18·2	
10·8	9·5	8·2	7·1			6·5	
81·5	43·5	18·8	9·0			7·9	
6·0	4·8	3·8	2·8			2·6	

		FF	C	c
21	Anonymous clavichord, *c.* 1700 C/E–c³, fretted, double-strung 8¹			90·2	75·0
22	Clavichord by Hass, 1763 FF–f³, unfretted, double-strung 8¹ c–f³, triple-strung 8¹ 8¹ 4¹ FF–b				
		8¹	147·3	132·7	103·2
		4¹	112·4	92·0	62·6 (b
23	Clavichord by Dolmetsch, 1896 FF–f³, unfretted, double-strung 8¹ c♯–f³, triple-strung 8¹ 8¹ 4¹ FF–c				
		8¹	139·7	132·1	101·3
		4¹	110·5	91·6	60·3

String Scales of the Pianofortes

		FF	C	c
24	Grand pianoforte by Backers, 1772 FF, GG–f³, double-strung	175·3	161·3	101·3
25	Square pianoforte by Rochead, *c.* 1805 FF–c⁴, double-strung, fourteen lowest overspun	138·5	121·9	88·3
26	Cabinet upright pianoforte by Broadwood, 1834 CC–c⁴, double-strung	152·3	148·8	137·9

c^1	c^2	c^3	f^3	
48·9	26·0	12·7		
55·9	28·5	14·0	10·2	
56·5	28·2	13·5	10·5	

c^1	c^2	c^3	f^3	c^4
51·8	26·0	13·5	10·2	
55·2	29·2	14·0		7·0
106·8	56·0	29·0	14·2	7·6

Harpsichord Action «SINGLE ACTION»

Virginals and spinets have a similar action,
differing only in certain details.

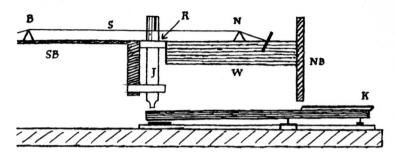

cross-section

B = BRIDGE. J = JACK. K = KEY.
N = NUT. NB = NAMEBOARD.
R = REGISTER, HOLDING JACK IN PLACE.
S = STRING. SB = SOUNDBOARD.
W = WRESTPLANK.

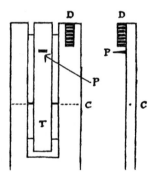

Enlargement of jack, front and side

C = CENTRE PIN, HOLDING TONGUE IN PLACE.
D = DAMPER. P = PLECTRUM, (PROTRUDING).
T = TONGUE.

Clavichord Action

K = KEY. T = TANGENT OF METAL.
S = DOUBLE STRINGS, RUNNING ALMOST
PARALLEL TO KEYBOARD-FRONT.
D = DAMPING FELT.

Pianoforte Action
Broadwood's Grand Action, simplified

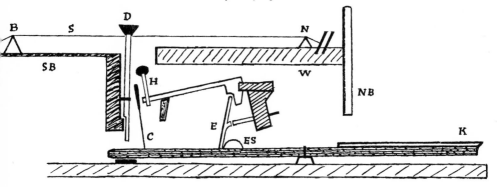

B = BRIDGE. C = CHECK. D = DAMPER.
E = ESCAPEMENT. ES = ESCAPEMENT SPRING.
H = HAMMER. K = KEY. N = NUT.
NB = NAMEBOARD. S = STRING, (DOUBLE).
SB = SOUNDBOARD. W = WRESTPLANK.

Chamber Organ Action

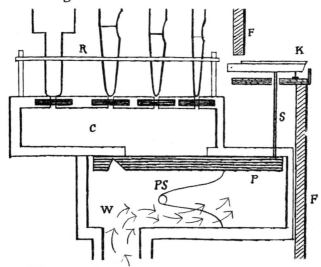

C = CHEST. F = FRONT OR CASE OF ORGAN.
K = KEY. P = PALLETT. PS = PALLETT SPRING.
R = RACK ('FALSE SOUNDBOARD').
S = STICKER FROM KEY TO PALLETT.
W = WIND FROM BELLOWS.